HIDDEN

TREASURES

*Finding the **'Hidden Treasures'** of God*

*Featuring the author's
personal testimony*

Marilyn McGruder

Dedication

This book is dedicated to my loving husband, Greg McGruder, my precious family and dearest friends. You believed in me and encouraged me from *Day One*. I thank God for you all every day.

I would also like to thank my church family, Hopewell Missionary Baptist Church in Pompano Beach, Florida for your continued support. With a special thank you to my pastor, Dr. Robert Stanley and his lovely wife, Sister Alene Stanley and all of the other great ministers for their truly anointed teaching of God's Word.

Contents

Marilyn's Story:

It all began when I was just a naïve 14-year-old high school girl. A boy introduced himself to me. I thought he was cute, and he seemed nice at first, but as time went on, he would abuse me emotionally, physically, and financially.

This horrible relationship set up a pattern that continued long after we both graduated from high school. Since he was my first relationship, I never learned how to stand up for myself and I was too afraid to fight back or even tell my family. It's crazy, but I blamed myself, maybe for getting into the relationship in the first place. But it wasn't my fault. He fooled me and everybody and I was too ashamed to face the reality of my situation. On the outside, he was a happy, fun-loving and incredibly handsome man. But in private, he became a different person: wicked and controlling. Later, I learned his father was also abusive, so that's likely where he picked up the habit of abuse and control.

To cope, I turned to alcohol and then he introduced me to cocaine and marijuana. I did anything to ease the pain and get along. Despite having my consciousness numbed with drugs, alcohol, and abuse, I knew there was more for me than this and I had to do something. I kept hope alive, thinking that things would get better; but instead, his anger towards me escalated. We were together for **several years** when my depression, anger, and rage built to a point to where I knew I was either going to take my life or his. Yes, I felt like I had to kill him, or I was never going to be FREE! Not only that, I had no doubt in my mind that if I left him alive, he would hurt another innocent young woman. Somehow, I grabbed hold of myself and didn't take such drastic measures. A piece of advice for anyone reading this who's feeling like you are in a similar situation, keep a log in a safe place for when you have the strength to leave or get help. I'm so grateful that I did not kill myself or him. Something spoke to me. I believe that something was God.

You see, even during this very dark and depressed season of my life, I felt the presence of God there with me the whole time. I had a Bible! My King James Bible had a pink leather cover. I don't know where it came from, but when I was hurting bad, I would go read it in private. I was drawn to it. And when I read it, I received comfort and I believed what GOD said inside. I began to ask and pray for God to come and get me and save me from that place. One day, God instilled in me the strength and courage to do just that. The plan was simple. You might wonder why I hadn't done it before. I took my fiancé's keys and his car, and I fled to my parents' home for safety, never to turn back. The keys were there the whole time. It was God's Word that gave me the courage to escape, to change my entire life.

Still to this day, I THANK JESUS for saving my life from a living hell. I cried out to Him, and He came-just as He promised in the Bible. Yes, I still have some residual scars from the abuse, in the form of occasional anxiety and/or Post-Traumatic Stress Disorder (PTSD). But I'm still here and in the race for a much better ME. By the grace of God, I'm not on any medication.

I created this 21 Day journal to help others gain the strength through God that I had. I believe that it was the love of my family who kept me in prayer that drew me to that little pink Bible. That Bible was my hidden treasure. If it wasn't for that foundation and my Bible, I don't believe I would have survived. I'd like to be that foundation for you with this journal. I'd like to help you find your hidden treasure.

I know what it feels like to be rejected and neglected. I am familiar with being used and abused, pushed aside, and ignored. I remember when he tried to make me feel like I didn't matter, like I was unimportant, and without feelings. If you've been there or are there now, I just want you to know that you are also very important to GOD because everything God creates has a special purpose (God don't make junk!!!). We all have a specific purpose that God wants us to realize. He will help you to figure out what "THAT" is. As you go through this 21-Day journey like I did (Yes, I went through the devotional before you), I ask you to believe in the Spirit of God who created you as He guides you to a good and expected end.

This Is What God Says About YOU in His Word.... You are a chosen race, a royal priesthood, a dedicated Nation, God's Own purchased, special people, that you may set forth the wonderful deeds and display the virtues and perfections of Him who called you out of Darkness Into His Marvelous Light. 1 Peter 2:9

In closing, it is my desire that you will begin to see the power of Jesus' spirit or "Hidden Treasure" within you which will lead you and guide you to living your dreams and helping others to reach theirs. Don't be afraid to be GREAT-God needs YOU!

****

Why Me???
"Poetry from The Heart"
by Cynthia Folston-Williams

Going along as free as can be, fulfilling a dream walking in Ministry,

Preaching, praying, and prophesying, watching people get delivered-some laughing, some crying.

Suddenly, you go through tests and trials throughout the years, some things so bad it brings you to tears. You know in your heart you just want to be free, crying out to God saying, "Lord, why me? I did everything You asked me to do; if You needed me to do more, I would have done that too." You get to church early and many times, leave late, taking care of everything so the people wouldn't have to wait. You watch some preachers lie, cheat, and steal, while deceiving the people making them believe it's God's will.

You just ponder in your heart because it's hard to believe, how some get away with these Wicked Deeds. When God has a purpose in store for you, HE allows a series of events to happen that you have to go through. But don't you panic, just remember it's a test, all of those events are part of your process. He wouldn't put more on us than we can bear, and when it's all over, we'll realize how much HE cares. At the end of the test there is a light, so I encourage you to stay in the ring– and fight for what's right! The next time you cry out Lord, "Why me?" When you look back over your life, you'll be surprised at what you see. So, don't give up and don't you give in, when it's all said and done, you will win in the end.

Section I: Who are You?
My history does not define my destiny.

Day 1 - The Consummation of God's Love

1 John 4:19 We love Him because He first loved us. - NKJV

Perhaps you thought you had to be good enough or someone with special gifts and talents to have God's love-but God's love is a FREE gift, a "hidden treasure" that is unconditionally yours. It comes to us through the sacrifice that Jesus made when HE died for all of us on the cross. Receive It!

Prayer: Father God I thank You for Your love right now in Jesus' name. I believe that You love me, and You sent Your Son to die just for me. I receive Your love today and I pray that it sets me free. Jesus please forgive me of all my sins, and I ask You to help my heart with unbelief.

Notes:

Notes:

Day 2 - Cast Down but Not Conquered

2 Corinthians 4:7-9 But we have this treasure in Earthen vessels that the excellence of the power may be of God and not of us. We are hard-pressed on every side, yet not crushed. We are perplexed, but not in despair; persecuted but not forsaken, struck down but not destroyed. – NKJV.

I thank God that when I read this Scripture, I knew without a shadow of a doubt that because He is on the inside of us– our "hidden treasure" –we can never be destroyed. This gives me joy, peace, and confidence to live every day, as best I can, in HIS power no matter my successes, or failures and life's ups and downs.

Prayer: Father God I thank You for keeping me. You have protected me, and You have provided for me because I know that Your power and Your spirit lives on the inside of me. You give me strength to live, to fight every battle, and to face every fear. Even when I feel weak, I know that I am really strong. Teach me to draw from the "hidden treasure" You placed on the inside of me, in Jesus' name I pray. AMEN.

Notes:

Notes:

Day 3 – God's Plans for You

Jeremiah 29:11 For I know the plans I have for you, declares the LORD, plans to prosper you and not to harm you, plans to give you a hope and a future. NIV

Lord I thank You that Your plans for me are good and great.

Prayer: Lord help me to keep my mind stayed on the plans that You have for my life and not only on the plans that I want because Your plans for me are so much more that I could have ever imagined. Amen.

Notes:

Notes:

Day 4 – God Choose You

Ephesians 2:10 For we are God's workmanship, created in Christ Jesus to do good works, which GOD prepared in advance for us to do. NIV

2 Corinthians 5:17 Therefore, if anyone is in Christ, he is a new creation; the old has gone, the new has come! NIV

My my...I thank God that He can make us all brand new. This is a miracle.

Prayer: Father God I thank You for a new day and a new season to be made over and brand-new with the same Mind and Spirit as You in Jesus' name Amen.

Notes:

Notes:

Day 5 - Having a Godly Spirit

Colossians 3:12 Therefore, as God's chosen people, holy and dearly loved, clothe yourselves with compassion, kindness, humility, gentleness, and patience.

Lord, I Thank You that your Bible is an instructional manual which describes how we are to resemble Your Spirit.

Prayer: Father God please help me to be full of Your Spirit....to be full of Your kindness, compassion, humility, gentleness, patience, and your love. That's what I want to be in Jesus' name. Amen.

Notes:

Notes:

Section II: Who am I? The Great "I am."

GOD created the heavens and the earth and all therein.

Day 6 - The "Hidden Treasure"

Luke 12:34 "For where your treasure is, there your heart will be also." – NKJV

When I read this Scripture, it reminds me that God is the best treasure we could ever find. We must continue to take care of something that's so valuable and keep Him close to our hearts. As you keep God close, you will find that the "Hidden Treasure" is your true power source!

Prayer - Lord, as I seek Your face today, I ask You to keep my mind stayed on Thee and off all my problems, worries, and any distractions that could come between You and me. Lord, I ask You to give me clarity of mind and heart and point me in the right direction in order to serve You now and even after these 21 days. Please forgive me of my sins. It's in the mighty name of Your Son Jesus that I pray. AMEN.

Notes:

Notes:

Day 7 - God's Perfection

<u>Psalm 36:7</u> How precious is Your loving kindness, oh God! Therefore, the children of men take refuge and put their trust Under The Shadow of Your Wings. - NKJV
If King David could be confident in God's love when he wrote this scripture, then we also can trust and be confident in God's love for us as well.

Prayer: Father God I thank You today for your unfailing love. It has been with me since the beginning. I thank You dear Lord and I believe by faith that it is because of Your love I will develop and fully grow into the individual You sent me here to be... it's in Jesus' name that I pray Amen.

Notes:

Notes:

Day 8 - The Eternal Faithfulness of the Lord

Psalm 105:1-3 Oh, give thanks to the LORD! Call upon His name. Make known His deeds among the peoples! Sing to him, sing Psalms to Him; talk about his wondrous works! Glory To His holy name; let the hearts of those Rejoice who seek the Lord! - NKJV

The Bible says that GOD is looking for those who will praise HIM and worship HIM. Do you
even tell people how good God has been to you? How He brought you out of the bondage in your mind, from your fears, from alcohol, drug abuse, and any other problems you know you could not have resolved by yourself.

Prayer: Lord you have been so good to me, better than I could ever be to myself. I thank You for Your undying faithfulness and protection. When I was at my lowest point, You picked me up. I will continue to give You all the praise. In Jesus' name I pray. AMEN.

Notes:

Notes:

24

Day 9 - Jesus Counsels the rich young ruler

Matthew 19:21 JESUS said to him, "...if you want to be perfect, go, sell what you have and give to the poor, and you will have treasure in heaven, and come, follow me." - NKJV

Ahhh, there's that word again. When we follow Jesus, we will certainly have Treasures stored up in Heaven for those who believe that Jesus is real - even blessings given to us here and now.

Prayer: Father God I thank You on today that Your Son is real. He is here with us; He is providing for us each and every day. Amen and Amen.

Notes:

Notes:

Day 10 – You Can Trust GOD

<u>Proverbs 3:5-6</u> Trust in the Lord with all your heart and lean not on your own understanding; in all your ways acknowledge Him and he will make your paths straight. - NIV

Every time I read this Scripture, I thank GOD for getting me back on course and in line with Him because most times when I depend on myself, I generally come to the wrong conclusions – which could eventually hurt me or someone close to me that I love and care about.

Prayer: Father God, this is the day that You have made. I shall rejoice and be glad in it. I ask You Lord to help me keep my mind stayed on Thee and not to lean on my own understanding because when I do, I sometimes get myself into trouble. In Jesus' name I pray AMEN and AMEN.

Notes:

Notes:

Section III: How can I help you?

Day 11 – Call on Me

Psalm 50:15 Call upon Me in the day of trouble; I will deliver you, and you shall glorify Me. – NKJV

As you read this Scripture, you will come to see that God is with you, and He will protect you. Yes, we all will go through some difficult times, but He is still there to help us through them all.

Prayer: Father God on today I thank You that I am special in Your eyes. I am Your child and You are my Father and You care about everything that bothers me, hinders me or hurts me. I shall glorify You always, in Jesus' name I pray.

Notes:

Notes:

Day 12 - The Parable of the Hidden Treasure

<u>**Matthew 13:44**</u> The Kingdom of Heaven is like a "treasure hidden" in a field, which a man found and hid, and for Joy over it he goes and sells all that he has and buys that field.

The Kingdom of Heaven is so very precious that God describes it as a "Hidden Treasure" because it is of GREAT value. We must take heed to know what we should love and seek.

Prayer: Father God, on this day I ask You to help me to understand the value of Heaven and the price that You had to pay to get me there. I don't fully understand its worth, but please help me to stay on the path of righteousness for Your namesake. In Jesus' name I pray, AMEN.

Notes:

Notes:

Day 13 - A Heavenly Inheritance

1 Peter 1:5-6 Through faith we are kept by the power of God for salvation ready to be revealed in the last times. In this you greatly Rejoice, though now for a little while, if need be, you have been grieved by various trials, that the genuineness of your faith being much more precious than gold that perishes, though it is tested by fire may be found praise, honor, and Glory at the revelation of Jesus Christ.

Our amazing God will take care of and keep His children safe from destruction until the day of our salvation. Not only that, we can rejoice now even with this life and its troubles.

Prayer: Father God, I thank You that You are my provider, my keeper, my teacher, my friend and my strong tower. I don't have to worry or be afraid from living in these harsh times because my salvation is secure. In Your Son's name I pray, Amen.

Notes:

Notes:

Day 14 - The Confession of our Sins

1 John 1:9 If we confess our sins, HE is faithful and just and will forgive us our sins and purify us from all unrighteousness.

AMEN and AMEN! I thank GOD that it is just that simple. The Love of GOD compels us to look at our lives and ask for His forgiveness on today so that we can live victoriously. When I first read that–I believed, and so can you! Repent and be baptized from all our sins. We all have fallen short on a daily basis.

Prayer: Lord, on today I thank You for the simple act of confessing my sins in order to live a more powerful and successful life. Please forgive me on today Dear GOD of all my sins and please show me those things that I am not aware of that could be hurting my life, my relationships, and a closer walk with YOU. In your Son's name, Jesus, I pray. Amen.

Notes:

Notes:

Day 15 - True Beauty, a Quiet and Humble Spirit

<u>1 Peter 3:3-4</u> Do not let your adornment be merely outward, arranging the hair, wearing gold, or putting on fine apparel. Rather let it be the "hidden person of the heart," with The Incorruptible beauty of a gentle and quiet Spirit, which is very precious in the sight of God.

I many times get this wrong, thinking that I'm being humble but not taking the time to pay attention to my outward behavior. Not trying to be prideful on purpose but missing the mark which GOD wants on display.

Prayer: Father GOD, please help me to have a humble loving and kind spirit like Jesus. Lord I give You permission to change me, mold me and make me over and please don't stop talking to me. Thank You Father, Amen.

Notes:

Notes:

Day 16 - The Redeemer of Israel

Isaiah 43:1-3 The Lord who created me says, don't be afraid, for I have ransomed you. I have called you by name, and you are mine. When you go through deep Waters and great trouble, I will be with you. When you go through rivers of difficulty, you will not drown! When you walk through the fire of Oppression, you will not be burned up, the flames will not consume you. For I am the Lord your God, your savior, the Holy One of Israel. –TLB

God says that when you go through horrible and difficult times, as we believe on Him, as we believe on His Son Jesus, we will not be destroyed and we will not be consumed by our troubles or difficult situations because He is our God, Our protector, and Our Redeemer. AMEN.

Prayer: Father God, on today, I thank You for being my provider and protector at all times, even when it feels like I'm not going to make it through. I thank You that you are aware of every situation that I'm dealing with right now and in my future. As I turn it all over to You, I will not be consumed. Please increase my faith. In Jesus' name I pray. Amen.

Notes:

Notes:

Section IV: Special scriptures to remember:

Day 17 - The Value of Wisdom

Proverbs 2:1-5 My son/daughter, if you receive my words, and treasure my commands within you, so that you incline your ear to wisdom, and apply your heart to understanding; Yes, if you cry out for discernment, and lift up your voice for understanding, if you seek her as silver, and search for her as for Hidden Treasures; then you will understand the fear of the Lord, and find the knowledge of God. - NKJV

This is kind of a long Scripture but so important to the Christian life. God wants us to see the value of having wisdom and living as best we can in keeping His commandments, then we can hopefully understand the greatest commandment of all-love the Lord your God/Jesus with all your heart, mind, and soul and to love your neighbor as yourself.

Prayer: On this day Dear Lord, I ask You for knowledge, wisdom, and understanding to receive Your Word and have a strong desire to study the Word and to seek Your face. Then I may be worthy to know and to begin to understand the fear of the Lord. It's in Your Son's name I pray, AMEN.

Notes:

Notes:

Day 18 - The Compassionate High Priest

Hebrews 4:15 For we do not have a High Priest who cannot sympathize with our weaknesses, but was in all points tempted as we are, yet he was without sin.
Lord we thank you for understanding all of our problems and yet with your divine grace and mercy.

Prayer: Father God, Thank You today for understanding me and my problems, yet having compassion and giving me grace and mercy daily. Lord, help me to have the same heart of love and compassion for another. In Jesus' name, Amen.

Notes:

Notes:

Day 19 - A Book of Remembrance

Malachi 3:17 "They shall be mine," says the Lord of hosts, "On the day that I make them my jewels and I will spare them as a man spares his own son who serves him." - NKJV

As you read this Scripture, you will come to see that as you serve the Lord and stay committed to Him, you are a precious jewel in His eyes, and He will cover you.

Prayer: Father God, on today I thank You that I am special in Your eyes. I'm a special Jewel that You set aside for Your purposes. I ask You to help me to see me through Your eyes and that I may stay on the righteous path for Your namesake - in Jesus' name Amen.

Notes:

Notes:

Day 20 - The new heaven and the new earth

Revelation 21:18-21 The material of the wall was jasper and the city was pure gold, like clear glass. The foundation stones of the city wall were adorned with every kind of precious stone. The first foundation stone was jasper; the second, sapphire; the third, chalcedony; the fourth, emerald. And the twelve gates were twelve pearls; each one of the gates was a single pearl. And the street of the city was pure gold, like transparent glass.

My thoughts: I've never seen Heaven in a dream or in the vision, but that doesn't mean it's not real - have you? My sister told me as a girl, God showed her Heaven in a dream and her description was quite like what the Bible says. I believe God's Word. He's done enough in my life through my faith and the power of prayers, and I will continue to trust and believe unless someone can prove HIM wrong.

Prayer: Father God we thank You for a new Heaven and a new Earth that we will be able to experience Heaven someday and there be no fear in death in Jesus' name we pray AMEN.

Notes:

Notes:

Day 21 - Thankfulness and Prayer

Philippians 1:6 Being confident of this very thing, that HE who has begun a good work in you will complete it until the day of Jesus Christ. - NKJV.

As you read this Scripture, you will come to see that God is not through with us yet. HE will be continually making us over and over again as we stay close to HIM.

Prayer: Father God on today, I thank You that all my brothers and sisters are special in Your eyes. According to our faith and belief and prayer for coming to the same place, as You make us over and to be more like Your Son Jesus. Thank you, Lord, thank you! We can never thank You enough. Amen, Amen and AMEN.

Notes:

Notes:

Reflective Thoughts

Reflective Thoughts

Reflective Thoughts

Reflective Thoughts

<u>Reflective Thoughts</u>

Reflective Thoughts

Reflective Thoughts

Reflective Thoughts

Reflective Thoughts

Reflective Thoughts

Reflective Thoughts

Reflective Thoughts

ABOUT THE AUTHOR

Marilyn Maurita McGruder is a Motivational Speaker, Author, and the Founder of Hidden Treasure Foundation, Incorporated, a non-profit company located in South Florida geared towards assisting the homeless. She believes that helping the homeless population can help change the nation because all people have a hidden treasure on the inside.

Marilyn is a graduate of the Fort Lauderdale College with a degree in Business Admin. She is employed as a paralegal with the Federal Government and a member of Toastmasters. For ten years, Marilyn served as a youth counselor and speaker at her home church.

The three books that changed Marilyn's life were the *Holy Bible*, *The Power of Positive Thinking* by Norman Vincent Peale, and *Woman Thou Art Loosed* by T. D. Jakes. These books brought about a drastic transformation and change in her life.

Marilyn is a survivor of Domestic Violence and currently advocates for women and children who are homeless as a result of abuse. She loves to spend time with her family and close friends but especially with her husband, Greg, and their Jack Russell, Pepper.

You can contact Marilyn at
HiddenTreasueFoundation@yahoo.com
Phone number 954-300-3455

www.ingramcontent.com/pod-product-compliance
Lightning Source LLC
Chambersburg PA
CBHW060145050426
42448CB00010B/2312